BEFORE YOU HIRE A CFO

8 Disciplines to Increase
Financial Visibility and Control

Troy D. Schrock

TABLE OF CONTENTS

INTRODUCTION

Imagine driving a car with the windshield so dirty and grimy that you can barely see the road ahead. Imagine driving that same car, with the same dirty windshield, at 180 mph. Now imagine driving that car with your only visibility being a small rearview mirror. Are you comfortable? What are your chances of successfully driving at *slow* speeds, let alone normal traffic or racing speeds?

This example identifies an important lesson:

> *The more limited your visibility, the more slowly you must proceed and the less likely you are to be successful.*

Despite this simple lesson, many business owners run their organizations with very limited visibility. They may periodically inspect financial statements and ratios, but these results, like a rearview mirror, are lagging indicators of performance, measuring activity that is, at best, a few weeks old. Financial statements and the resulting ratios are certainly important, but they provide little to no forward visibility and control. Relying exclusively on them impedes business growth and, more seriously, jeopardizes the business's very existence.

Why Businesses Fail

Unsurprisingly, financial factors top nearly every list of reasons why businesses fail. Descriptions such as "undercapitalization," "lack of financial understanding," or something similar, are simply different labels for the same problem: running out of cash. A business can perform strongly based on financial indicators such as revenue growth, market share, gross margin and profitability, yet still run out of cash.

Running out of cash sometimes results from the business growing too quickly. However, "growing too quickly" is actually a euphemism for growing faster than the owner's ability to see and react appropriately. In other words, the owner lacks financial visibility and control. While it might appear the business grew so quickly that it ran out of capital, the reality is that adequate financial control systems were not implemented, leaving the owner to drive with only a grimy windshield and a rearview mirror. With better systems, he or she could have anticipated obstacles and reacted accordingly – perhaps raising more capital or cutting costs – before hitting a crisis.

Raising capital is always more difficult and costly during a cash crunch, especially if the business owner never saw it coming. With all the tools, systems, and knowledge available to business owners today, such miscalculations are inexcusable. Yet time and again, businesses fail to anticipate gross margin, profitability, and cash flow because they simply do not have adequate forecast systems in place. This always results in underperformance, and sometimes, failure.

Resource for Business Owners

Before You Hire a CFO is written especially for business owner CEOs who are contemplating one of the following:

- Hiring a full-time CFO
- Dealing with an underperforming CFO
- Improving systems to increase financial visibility and control

Businesses facing these issues typically generate from $2 million to $20 million in annual revenue and employ from 30 to 300 people. At this size, the business begins to take on the unique characteristics of a mid-size business. The business owner is usually the CEO, and the rigors of the business require that 100% of his or her time be devoted to that role. Other roles, such as sales oversight, marketing, finance, information technology, human resources, and operations, must be delegated to capable individuals.

Unfortunately, the CFO role, usually viewed as not being customer-focused or revenue-generating, is often among the last to be delegated to a qualified professional. The CEO may find it difficult to justify an annual investment of $100,000 to $180,000 (salary, bonuses, payroll taxes, and benefits) for a CFO position. Instead, the CEO assumes the role of CFO. This dual role will impede business growth and endanger the organization's existence, for no matter how good he or she is, no one has the bandwidth to perform both functions in a mid-size business.

What most CEOs don't realize is that an effective financial management system can be implemented that provides the visibility and control required to grow the business *without requiring a full-time CFO* or the CEO to operate as one.

Before You Hire a CFO provides CEOs of mid-size businesses with the required knowledge to implement a financial visibility and control system like those used by much larger, more sophisticated companies. This forestalls, sometimes for years, the need to hire a full-time CFO, yet still delivers the financial management system that is so critical to success. For business owners who already have a CFO, this book will help them understand what information and disciplines their CFO should be providing them.

Existing Resources

The list of books and materials addressing financial matters for business is extensive, but most target small business owners or financial managers in large organizations. Few address the needs of mid-size businesses. *Before You Hire a CFO* endeavors to fill this niche. Focused specifically on the needs of mid-size business owners, it emphasizes the implementation of a disciplined financial management system.

The Layout

This book is divided into three sections:

- **Section 1** lays the groundwork for understanding the purpose and measurement of a comprehensive financial management system.
- **Section 2** presents eight disciplines necessary for financial visibility and control.
- **Section 3** identifies the benefits of a part-time CFO advisor and offers recommended resources for continued learning.

After completing all three sections, you will better understand the importance of a financial visibility and control system. More importantly, you will have the information and perspectives necessary to implement such a system in your business.

Are you ready to learn how to improve financial visibility and control in your business?

Others Who May Find This Resource Valuable

This book may also be of value to other business professionals, including:

- Financial advisors and CPAs who provide part-time CFO services
- Commercial lenders
- Investment bankers

Any of these may encounter a business that lacks an effective financial management system. In this book, financial advisors will find information and guidance to help deliver CFO services to mid-size business owners. Commercial lenders and investment bankers will find a practical tool to share with clients lacking solid financial management. Such clients can then be encouraged to implement this system themselves, or they can be referred to a CFO advisor who will implement the system for them.

Thank you for choosing *Before You Hire a CFO* for your mid-size business. I am confident you will find this book both relevant and informative.

Best regards,

Troy D. Schrock, CPA
CFO Advisor and developer of The Action CFO Process™
January 2008

UNDERSTANDING THE
FOUR BOTTOM LINES
1

The most common "bottom line" of business measurement is net profit (net income). However, net profit is only one of *four* bottom lines indicating the true financial performance of a company; in fact, it's not even the most important.

The four bottom lines that a CEO must fully understand and monitor are:

- Return on Invested Capital
- Net Profit
- Operating Cash Flow
- Profit Per Employee

Each of these measures a distinct aspect of the business. Every metric has inherent limitations and weaknesses, and these four are no exception. Considering these four metrics as a complete package, however, provides a complete view of "bottom line performance" with which to evaluate the health of the business.

In *Managing By The Numbers*, noted business authors Chuck Kremer and Ron Rizzuto make the case for three distinct bottom lines. Two elements differentiate my recommendations from theirs. First, I use *return on invested capital* instead of *return on assets*. Second, I include *profit per employee*, a metric I feel is more in tune with mid-size businesses that rely heavily on contributions from talented people rather than tangible assets.

Return on Invested Capital

If forced to choose the most important of the four bottom lines, it would likely be *return on invested capital*. This measure demonstrates how successfully the business enterprise turns capital (resources) into profit. In other words, it measures how effectively the company uses its money (borrowed or owned). After all, the primary financial reason for a business to exist is to return profit to capital holders (investors and lenders). To be considered a strong performer, a business must at least yield a return higher than its cost of capital.

Return on Invested Capital

$$\frac{\text{Net Profit} + \text{Interest} + \text{Amortization}}{\text{Total Assets - Excess Cash - Non-Interest-Bearing Current Liabilities}}$$

Non-interest-bearing current liabilities are essentially trade accounts payable, accrued liabilities, and deferred revenue.

The denominator of this formula is based on the balance sheet, but with net profit as the prime input of the numerator, this measure is equally affected by revenue and expenses.

Return on invested capital is very useful when comparing the financial performance of different businesses, whether within or across industries. Every company generates different revenue, profit, and cash flow levels, but *return on invested capital* provides an equalizing measure of how effectively companies produce profit from a given base of resources.

If *return on invested capital* is such a good measure, why is it not the sole bottom line metric of business performance? As noted previously, every metric has inherent limitations, so it's not wise to rely on only one. The limitations of *return on invested capital* include:

- It does not measure cash flow.
- It can be easily manipulated using varied accounting methods.
- It is more difficult to measure than the other three bottom line measurements.

Net Profit

Net profit measures the economic reality of a value proposition over time. In other words, is the customer willing to pay more for the product or service than it costs the business to produce and deliver it? If so, the business will generate a net profit. This metric is calculated by deducting all operating expenses from total revenue (sales).

One must know the accrual basis and matching principle to fully understand *net profit*. Accrual basis *net profit* focuses on the promise and agreement aspect of a business transaction. In addition, capital items that are expensed over time (as depreciation) must be separated from normal expenses.

The inherent limitations of *net profit* include:

- It does not reveal the real cash situation since it focuses on the promise and agreement part of a business transaction.
- It is an abstract measure because it comes from the income statement and can be manipulated with different accounting methods.

Operating Cash Flow

Cash flow for a business is like fuel for a vehicle: it keeps the business running. A business can operate for awhile at a net loss, but it cannot operate one day without cash. *Operating cash flow* measures how much cash is generated by the operations of the business. This metric focuses on the cash settlement part of a transaction. Not included in *operating cash flow* are cash items related to capital investments (buildings, equipment, etc.), investors, or lenders. In general, *operating cash flow* should exceed *net profit*; however, *net profit* should ultimately be the largest component of *operating cash flow*. One exception would be in businesses in a continuous pattern of high growth where cash is needed to fund working capital, primarily accounts receivable and inventory.

The inherent limitations of *operating cash flow* include:

- Since it focuses on the settlement part of a business transaction, it can be manipulated by varied accounting practices and management decisions (such as paying vendors late, holding customer checks for deposit at a later date, etc.).
- It can be manipulated and increased at the expense of profit, as in the practice of factoring receivables (selling receivables up front for a discount).

Profit Per Employee

Profit per employee measures the returns on talent in addition to capital. In today's knowledge-based economy, measuring the financial performance of intangibles is more important than ever. Intangibles might include process knowledge, brands, customer bases, or any other form of intellectual capital (specialized knowledge and relationships). Large profits can be produced by creating intangibles, as we see in the proliferation of technology, service, and web-based businesses. These businesses require little investment in traditional capital, but large amounts of investment in people talent. *Profit per employee* provides a metric indicating a company's success in converting its raw talent into profits. It is calculated by dividing the *net profit* by the number of full-time equivalent employees engaged in the business operations.

The inherent limitations of *profit per employee*, similar to those of its numerator, *net profit*, include:

- It does not reveal the real cash situation.
- It is an abstract measure because it comes from the income statement and focuses on the promise and agreement part of a business transaction.
- It can be manipulated through management decisions to use part-time or contract staff in place of full-time employees. Determining the number of full-time equivalent employees is an exercise in estimation.

If interested in learning more about *profit per employee*, read *The New Metrics of Corporate Performance: Profit per Employee* by Lowell Bryan (discussed further in Chapter 13).

Summary

The four bottom lines discussed in this chapter represent different methods of viewing the performance of business operations. Certain businesses or industries may have different terms for them, but the underlying principle is universal: every business must make a profit, generate cash flow, and provide a financial return on its investment in both capital and talent. These four bottom lines should be used together rather than relying on just one or two, for each has inherent limitations which are complemented by the others.

While it's critical to understand these four bottom lines, we should note that all four are lagging indicators, measuring past performance. Past performance does not determine future success. Furthermore, each of these measures can be manipulated through accounting practices and management decisions to show better current performance at the expense of future performance. For example, delaying or reducing spending in research & development, marketing or staffing levels will make all four bottom lines look stronger in the short term, but it robs the business of success in the future.

So how should you approach the future? What measurements should you use? Future performance requires an understanding of the key leading indicator: value.

UNDERSTANDING VALUE   2

Value is the equivalent of *future* return on invested capital. The technical process to determine value is called Discounted Cash Flow and consists of two components: risk and operating cash flow. You must understand the interaction and the variable drivers of these two components, for that is the only way to maximize value and yield the highest *future* return on invested capital and talent.

The topic of value could occupy several chapters, but that is beyond the scope of this book. Instead, we will focus on a high-level understanding of value as the leading indicator of future returns on invested capital.

Value Vector

Let's start by looking at a simple illustration of how value is determined, something we call the Value Vector (Figure 2.1).

Every business has a certain risk assigned to its future performance. You can think of *risk* as the return investors would expect relative to the risk and return characteristics of other possible investments. For example, an investment in a business is considered more risky than an investment in government bonds. Similarly, an investment in a small business is generally considered more risky than an investment in a large business. In addition to risk characteristics, every business has an expected future operating cash flow. Different proxies of operating cash flow may be used in different situations, such as EBITDA (earnings before interest, taxes, depreciation and amortization) or operating income (net income before miscellaneous or unusual expenses). Value for any given business is simply the inverse of the risk multiplied by the expected future operating cash flow.

It a business has a determined risk level that would require an investor to achieve a 25% return and this particular business has an expected annual average operating cash flow of $100,000, the value of that business would be $400,000 [4 (the inverse of 25%) x $100,000]. In this example, the expected 25% return converts to a four times *multiple*. A three times multiple would yield a lower value due to a higher perceived risk by the investor who would need to return 33% on the investment. Similarly, if the investor's perceived risk is lower, maybe only expecting a 20% return, then it would be a five times multiple and yield a higher value for the business. In short, lowering the risk and/or increasing the operating cash flow increases the company's value. Raising the risk and/or decreasing the operating cash flow decreases the company's value.

Who determines the risk level and expected cash flow, and thus the value, of a business? Only a potential buyer can make that determination. Like any

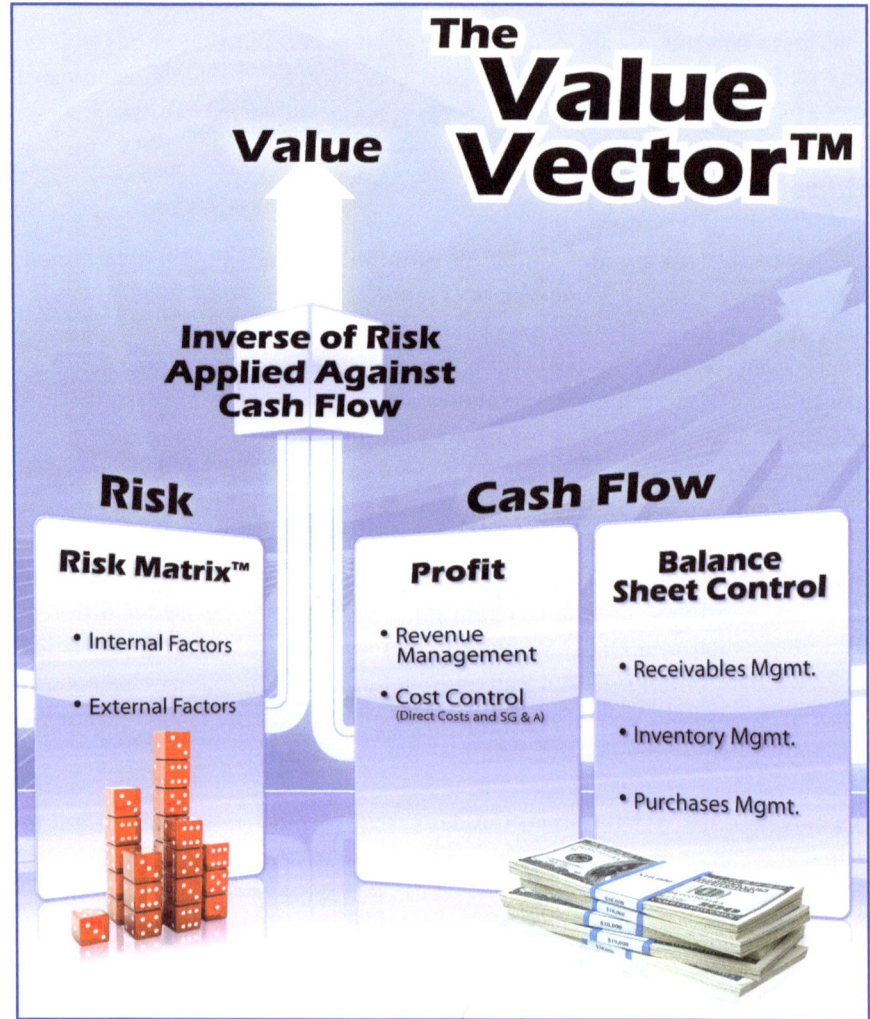

Figure 2.1

free-market transaction, it depends on what a buyer is willing to pay.

Each of the primary factors in determining value – risk and operating cash flow – have multiple drivers that create a unique interplay in any business. Let's consider those drivers in more detail.

Variable Drivers - Risk

The variable drivers of risk fall into two simple categories: internal risk factors and external risk factors. Internal risk factors include:

- Strength of the management team
- Diversity of the customer base
- Diversity of the revenue stream
- Revenue growth rate relative to industry growth rate
- Reliance on one or two key people
- Size relative to competitors

External risk factors include:

- State of the industry (growth, maturity or decline)
- Government regulation within the industry
- Competitive environment (low or high barriers to entry)
- Technology advances
- Global business environment
- Macroeconomic factors such as interest rates and money availability

These lists are far from comprehensive, but they provide a sampling of the types of risk characteristics investors consider. Like snowflakes, no two businesses are alike. No two businesses have the same risk complexion, and potential buyers will assess risk differently based on their present situations. Indeed, the value of a business complies with the old saying: "beauty is in the eye of the beholder."

Tom McKaskill's *Selling Your Business For a Premium* discusses how to identify buyers with the best "risk fit" to achieve the highest possible value for your business.

Variable Drivers - Operating Cash Flow

The variable drivers of operating cash flow fall into two categories: profit drivers and balance sheet control drivers.

Profit Drivers	Balance Sheet Control Drivers
Revenue Management Cost Control	Receivables Management Inventory Management Purchasing Management

The profit driver category includes revenue management and cost control. Revenue management ties back to value proposition pricing and promotion of a product or service, as well as systems to determine different prices for different customers based on quantity discounts or other factors. For example, airline companies use complex systems to maximize revenue across a broad range of customer needs.

Cost control includes both direct costs (cost of goods sold) and all other costs, including selling, general and administrative expenses. Clearly, a business cannot focus solely on cost control at the expense of actions necessary for revenue growth, but cost control plays a key role in maximizing operating cash flow. Every dollar in revenue only yields the contribution margin of that dollar to cash flow, but every dollar in cost savings yields that full dollar to cash flow. Therefore, time focused on cost control is time well spent.

In many respects, cost control is directly related to quality. For instance, a 4% error rate will consume 54% of the organization's resources – time, money, and creative energy. The staggering "cost of quality" is well documented, thanks to the 1990s advancement and implementation of Six Sigma and Lean Manufacturing knowledge.

The balance sheet control driver category includes three distinct variable drivers: receivables management, inventory management, and purchasing management, each of which directly impacts operating cash flow. For instance, your business might choose to implement a tight collection and accounts receivable review process that reduces average days outstanding of accounts receivable from 60 days to 45 days.

If interested in a more detailed review of cash flow drivers, we recommend *Cash Rules* by Bill McGuinness (discussed further in Chapter 13).

Interplay of the Variable Drivers of Risk and Operating Cash Flow

Decreasing risk factors and increasing operating cash flow simultaneously increases the value of your business. Sometimes, however, you must focus more heavily on one or the other. With no change to risk factors, improving cash flow will increase the value of your business. Similarly, your business might have no significant increase in cash flow, yet increase its value simply by mitigating one or more risk factors.

For example, if 50% of your revenue comes from one customer, you likely need to diversify your customer base. If you reach a point where no more than 10% of your revenue comes from any one customer while maintaining the same operating cash flow, your business will be perceived as less risky and therefore more valuable to a potential purchaser. Why? You have lowered the risk of a large financial impact to the future operating cash flow stream if you lose a customer.

In summary, the best way to increase the value of your business is to identify and implement strategic initiatives that both mitigate risk and increase operating cash flow.

OVERVIEW: FINANCIAL VISIBILITY AND CONTROL SYSTEM 3

The financial visibility and control system is a financial management system, producing the financial information necessary for better *understanding* and therefore increased *visibility* and *control*. Ultimately, a good financial visibility and control system leads to more effective decision-making by the CEO and executive team.

A *system* is effective because it is a repeatable set of processes that consistently delivers an expected result. People often avoid using any kind of system because of the time required to set up and learn. The initial time investment, however, is more than offset by the future time saved by effective decision-making. Indeed, the effectiveness of the system is measured by the intelligence it produces for the decision makers. Quality information is far more valuable than thick reports of useless data. The system's ability to produce valid information depends on its design and structure.

Clarifying a Financial Management System

A financial management system is a *set* of components; one component by itself is not a financial management system. For example, accounting software alone is not a financial management system. This may seem obvious, but many small and mid-size businesses install accounting software systems and think they have a financial management system. An accounting software package is merely a hygiene factor in a financial management system – necessary for producing accurate, timely financial statements.

Even generating accurate, timely financial statements does not indicate a financial management system. By themselves, financial statements do not yield much understanding; analysis of many elements is required to convert data to useful knowledge.

Financial statements by themselves have two additional limitations. First, they provide lagging data. Second, they are too infrequent. In today's fast-paced economic environment, timely decisions require much more frequent feedback than a monthly financial statement. Even so, you should not stop generating good financial statements as they are *one* of the components of a solid financial management system.

Key Disciplines of Financial Visibility and Control

A financial visibility and control system consists of eight key disciplines:

- Cash Flow Forecasting
- Smart Number Reporting
- Financial Statement Reporting
- Financial Analysis
- Narrative Financial Report
- Financial Advisory Review Meeting
- Financial Projections
- Bank or Investor Presentations

All eight disciplines work simultaneously, but I purposely place them in this sequence. The first two disciplines are very quick, simple steps that immediately extend financial visibility, much like new headlights.

Disciplines three through eight each require the output of the previous discipline to ensure proper execution. For example, discipline four, financial analysis, is a waste of time if discipline three, financial statement reporting, is not functioning properly. You must have timely, accurate financial statements in hand before beginning any kind of analysis.

Now, let's examine each discipline in detail.

DISCIPLINE 1:
CASH FLOW FORECASTING 4

THE OBJECTIVE

There is no more helpless feeling for a CEO than when the controller reveals an immediate need for additional cash in order to meet some financial obligation (payroll, for example). Everyone begins scrambling and reacting. When the cash need could have, and should have, been anticipated, an emergency call to the banker does not bode well for the business. The objective of cash flow forecasting, therefore, is to eliminate cash flow surprises by predicting cash flow activities three to four weeks ahead on a weekly basis.

CEOs are rightfully upset with cash flow surprises because it is relatively easy to anticipate and plan for a company's cash flow needs. All it requires is basic data analysis and regular communication to the CEO. The CEO must be constantly aware of cash flow needs for the business to be managed proactively.

GROWTH CONSUMES CASH

Why is cash flow so important? Cash is the fuel that keeps a business running. A business may be profitable and have plenty of assets, but without cash, it will go bankrupt. A large business may occasionally run out of cash, but most often it is small to medium-size businesses that run aground on this reef.

Why are small to medium-size businesses at greater risk? Put simply, growth consumes cash , and small to mid-size businesses generally grow more rapidly than large businesses on a percentage basis.

THE APPROACH

The primary tool for forecasting cash flow is a simple spreadsheet report. The process is not difficult, but it does require some additional time by your accounting personnel. It is common, in fact, for them to feel it should not be their job to prepare the cash flow forecast because it robs time from their other tasks.

The best way to overcome these objections is to make it clear that the information they prepare is critical to the company's success. Without it, the CEO lacks financial visibility and control. Hold them accountable for accurate, timely information and praise them when it occurs. They should know that their responsibility goes beyond recording data and processing transactions; they are to provide information essential to having financial visibility and control of the business.

The cash flow forecast process begins with a weekly routine (usually Monday morning) when the financial staff updates a spreadsheet report similar to that displayed in Figure 4.1. This routine consists of the following steps:

1. Review the check register from the prior week and update the Actual column in the spreadsheet (Figure 4.2), noting large variances from the Forecast.
2. Roll the new Actual Cash Balance number into the current week's Forecast Beginning Cash cell.
3. Review the current Accounts Receivable Aging report and forecast cash receipts for the current week and the next three to four weeks, based on due dates and knowledge of the customer's payment history.
4. Review the current Accounts Payable Aging report and forecast cash disbursements for the current week and the next three to four weeks, based on due dates and the company's payment cycle (some companies run payables only at mid-month and end-of-month).
5. Forecast cash disbursements for non-Accounts Payable items such as rent, payroll, payroll taxes, etc.
6. Forecast any cash flow activity related to fixed assets, financing, or shareholder transactions.
7. Update the latest line of credit formula (usually updated monthly based on the formula report submitted to the bank, which is based on receivables, inventory, etc.). Compare it to your current line of credit balance to determine the funds available at any given time.
8. For the current week, update the actual total outstanding common liabilities such as Accounts Payable (specifically noting how much is currently overdue), credit card liabilities and bank term debt.
9. Send the completed spreadsheet report to the CEO.

———— Prompt Attention to Collection Issues ————

The weekly cash flow forecast process and report offers a side benefit: it keeps you on top of accounts receivables collections.

The process allows you to see, on a weekly basis, a list of customers who have not paid as expected. This information prompts a call to the customer to check on payment status. In this way, many collections issues resulting from a lack of documentation, an invoice not received, or similar situations, are uncovered and addressed more quickly.

———————— Practical Tips ————————

1. Cash flow forecasting is a discipline that can easily slip in priority if left completely to accounting personnel. The forecasting and information reporting process requires time and effort by accountants, but it is much more meaningful to their CEO than it is to them. It is important for the CEO to periodically encourage accounting personnel by articulating the critical importance of the information they provide.

2. If your normal check run and payroll cycles are biweekly instead of weekly, you may choose to update the forecast biweekly. In this case, it's important to forecast three to four biweekly cycles instead of just three to four weeks.

3. Graphs quickly and easily present information. You can add a line graph to your spreadsheet to display the actual and forecast cash balances for the previous weeks as well as the forecast for upcoming weekly cash balances.

4. The CEO and financial personnel should not be too concerned with the detailed accuracy of the forecast. This is sometimes hard for financial staff because they are trained to be very accurate in everything they produce. Remember, though, that the objective of the cash flow forecast is to anticipate the next three to four weeks. It is an informed estimate. Everyone involved should remember the following:
   - Though actuals will vary from the forecast, the forecast is close enough to see the big picture and avert surprises
   - Forecasting is a learned skill. The more it is practiced, the easier it is to accurately perform.

XYZ COMPANY
Weekly Cash Flow Management Report

Week Ending July 31, 20____	Forecast	Actual	Variance
1) Beginning Cash on Hand			
Checking Account	$196,000		($196,000)
Total Beginning Cash Balance	**$196,000**		**($196,000)**
2) Cash Receipts			
Customer A	$32,000		($32,000)
Customer B	$18,000		($18,000)
Customer C	$56,000		($56,000)
Total Cash Receipts	**$106,000**		**($106,000)**
3) Cash Disbursements - Operations			
Cash Disbursements - Operations			
Vendor 1	($8,000)		$8,000
Vendor 2	($14,000)		$14,000
Others (small)	($6,000)		$6,000
Cash Disbursements - Payroll Wages and Taxes	($93,000)		$93,000
Total Cash Disbursements	**($121,000)**		**$121,000**
4) Net Operating Cash Activity	**($15,000)**		**$15,000**
5) Other Cash Activity			
Fixed Asset Purchases	($2,000)		$2,000
Bank Loan Payments			
Interest Payments on Bank Loans			
Shareholder Loans			
Other Total Cash Activity	**($2,000)**		**$2,000**
6) Total Cash Activity	**($17,000)**		**$17,000**
7) Total Ending Cash Balance	**$179,000**		**($179,000)**
8) Line of Credit - Per Formula	**$500,000**		**($500,000)**
9) Drawn on Line of Credit			
10) Line of Credit Available	**$500,000**		**($500,000)**

Key Variance Explanations
A=

Key Debt Information	
Accounts Payable	$123,000
Past Due Payables	$13,000
Term Bank Debt	$264,000

Figure 4.1: *Each week, the forecast should be updated for the upcoming three to four weeks. (Each sheet reflects one week's forecasted activity.)*

XYZ COMPANY
Weekly Cash Flow Management Report

Week Ending July 31, 20____	Forecast	Actual	Variance	
1) Beginning Cash on Hand				
Checking Account	$196,000	$196,000		
Total Beginning Cash Balance	$196,000	$196,000		
2) Cash Receipts				
Customer A	$32,000	$32,000		
Customer B	$18,000	$7,000	($11,000)	A
Customer C	$56,000	$58,000	$2,000	
Total Cash Receipts	$106,000	$97,000	($9,000)	
3) Cash Disbursements - Operations				
Cash Disbursements - Operations				
Vendor 1	($8,000)	($8,000)		
Vendor 2	($14,000)	($14,000)		
Others (small)	($6,000)	($5,000)	$1,000	
Cash Disbursements - Payroll Wages and Taxes	($93,000)	($92,000)	$1,000	
Total Cash Disbursements	($121,000)	($119,000)	$2,000	
4) Net Operating Cash Activity	($15,000)	($22,000)	($7,000)	
5) Other Cash Activity				
Fixed Asset Purchases	($2,000)	($3,000)	($1,000)	
Bank Loan Payments				
Interest Payments on Bank Loans				
Shareholder Loans				
Other Total Cash Activity	($2,000)	($3,000)	($1,000)	
6) Total Cash Activity	($17,000)	($25,000)	($8,000)	
7) Total Ending Cash Balance	$179,000	$171,000	($8,000)	
8) Line of Credit - Per Formula	$500,000	$500,000		
9) Drawn on Line of Credit				
10) Line of Credit Available	$500,000	$500,000		

Key Variance Explanations	
A=Paperwork missing - should be paid next week	

Key Debt Information	
Accounts Payable	$123,000
Past Due Payables	$13,000
Term Bank Debt	$264,000

Figure 4.2: *Each week, the actual activity for the prior week should be dropped in against the forecast. Then the new forecast can be made, refreshing the next two to three weeks and extending the forecast one more week.*

DISCIPLINE 2: 5
SMART NUMBER REPORTING

THE OBJECTIVE

The objective of Smart Number Reporting is to identify measures based on leading indicators and report them to decision-makers weekly, if not daily. Leading indicators are based on activities that ultimately lead to economic transactions, which in turn generate revenue and costs (financial results) for the business. When leading indicators are properly identified and measured, they provide reliable visibility of future results long before the financial statements report the actual results. Thus, we call them Smart Numbers.

THE APPROACH

Identify Your Smart Numbers

There are many ways to identify Smart Numbers. One way starts by identifying the top three to five key metrics in all functional areas of the business. From this list, management is usually able to identify three to five true leading indicators.

When searching for leading indicators, ask, "What tells me today that I'm having a good (or bad) month?" In other words, which activities, when performed well or at a certain volume, allow you to go home feeling good about the business? The answers may be activities that are not easy to measure; however, a reliable leading indicator is worth the time and resources necessary to measure and report the number.

Avoid the temptation to classify a whole slew of metrics as Smart Numbers. Instead, strive to develop a concise list. Carefully think through and clarify each metric so that the true leading indicators begin to emerge. For starters, six or seven Smart Numbers is enough to begin the reporting process, but after six to twelve months of practical use, you should target three to five.

Some general types of Smart Numbers should be used by most businesses. One is a view of the current revenue pipeline on a cumulative basis. For example, on a daily basis, you might show both the value of new contracts awarded yesterday and the value of new contracts waiting to be produced.

Another general type of Smart Number you should include is a measurement of your base economic unit of value. Every business has a base unit of economic value such as a billable hour or a finished product. It is important to know both the number of units produced and the number of units projected to be produced for a given time interval. For example, you might report the number of jobs in the shop today and the projected number of jobs in the shop each day for the next three days.

Another helpful Smart Number is one that reports how well you delivered on your value proposition the prior day/week. This, of course, is dependent on you knowing what your value proposition really is. Years ago, when next-day delivery by a "guaranteed time" was FedEx's commitment to customers, they monitored the number of times (not the percentage, which can be misleading depending on the number of transactions) they missed on their commitment each day and published the number across the organization the following morning.

The last general type of Smart Number might deal with cash – cash balance, cash flow, or funds available on the line of credit. Obviously, cash flow forecasting (Discipline 1) should be in place, but an appropriate cash-based Smart Number can provide a quick indicator of the company's cash comfort level.

———————— PRACTICAL TIP ————————

Business conditions change over time, so you should periodically review your Smart Numbers to ensure they are still applicable and appropriate. Sometimes a slight modification is required, while other times, one or two of the existing Smart Numbers may need to be replaced completely.

Smart Number Reporting Process

The Smart Number reporting process is as important as the Smart Numbers themselves. Information cannot inform decisions if not shared in a practical and useful way. A simple scorecard captures the Smart Numbers on a daily, or at least weekly, basis. In addition to providing the current Smart Number, the scorecard should provide context – the Smart Numbers for each day that week, the prior six weeks, or the last year, for example.

Who sees the Smart Number report is your decision. At the very least, the executive team should see the report. Other managers may benefit from seeing the overall company perspective contained in the Smart Number Report. Keep in mind, the purpose of Smart Numbers is to enable decision-makers to react quickly to the current reality. Everyone who can help the company by knowing the Smart Numbers should be included in the distribution.

──── SMART NUMBERS FROM DIFFERENT INDUSTRIES ────

Plus/Minus
Used in the staffing industry to measure the net increase or decrease in the number of working staff. A new employee starting in a contract position is a plus and an employee contract position that ends is a minus. In this case, revenue is a lagging indicator. After a quarter or two of consistent *plus*, we would expect to find revenue increasing on the monthly financial statements.

Gross Margin Percentage on New Contracts
This measure is used in many industries. An increasing trend in gross margin percentage on deals closed over the last week, month, or quarter should correspond to an increase in gross margin percentage on the income statement over time.

Number of Jobs in the Shop
Used in the printing industry to indicate current production volume. Individual jobs may be small or large, but this tends to even out over time. The executive team knows, for example, that if the number is less than ten, business is slow, but if it's more than twenty, business is good, given current staffing and equipment (capacity). This number paints a broad picture for expected revenue over a given period as well as production trends.

Number and Dollar Volume of Closings Booked
Used in homebuilding, real estate brokerage, mortgage, and title businesses. The number and dollar volume of closings completed or booked to close in a particular day, week, or month provides a direct view of upcoming revenue because it is generally booked on the calendar weeks before the actual financial transaction.

DISCIPLINE 3:
FINANCIAL STATEMENT REPORTING   6

THE OBJECTIVE

The objective of this discipline is to ensure that financial statements are produced both accurately and in a timely manner. Ideally, financial statements should be done by the 10th to the 15th of the month. With a reliable financial staff and accounting system, this should be no problem.

You need three basic financial statements: the Balance Sheet, Income Statement, and Cash Flow Statement. These standard documents will communicate the prior month's results to any experienced reader. Remember, financial statements are designed only to report historical performance. However, their usefulness is amplified when they serve as a stepping stone to disciplines four through six.

THE APPROACH

When completing the trial balance and closing out the accounting period, use the Balance Sheet Tie-Out Approach. Once the trial balance is properly tied out, it only takes a few mouse-clicks in the accounting software to generate the Income Statement and Balance Sheet. The Cash Flow Statement initially requires a bit more work because it is not included in the accounting system. Once a useful spreadsheet is designed, however, inputting data from the Balance Sheet and Income Statement is relatively quick and easy.

The Balance Sheet Tie-Out Approach is a method for ensuring that each Balance Sheet account (the assets, liabilities, and equity accounts) agrees with an outside detail or reconciliation of the period being reviewed. Specifically:

- Bank account balances (checking and savings) should match the bank statement after reconciling the register.
- The accounts receivable balance should tie to the detail accounts receivable aging schedule.
- Fixed asset details and the corresponding accumulated depreciation should match a detailed fixed asset schedule and depreciation schedule.

- Accounts payable balance should tie to the detail accounts payable aging schedule.
- Bank loans should agree with bank loan balance statements.

This process is applied to every Balance Sheet account. When completed, you should have a statement verifying every balance sheet account in the trial balance.

A clear activity cut-off is key to a good Balance Sheet tie-out. To record a transaction appropriately, you must be sure of the period in which it belongs. For example, where do you record a liability for something purchased and received but for which you have not yet received an invoice? Similar timing issues will arise in various places, so you should develop key questions and systems to help catch them for proper recording.

ACCOUNTING SOFTWARE SYSTEMS

Is there a particular accounting software system you should use? How robust of a system do you need? The answers to these questions are based on a number of key variables, such as:

- Complexity of your trial balance
- Number of departments or business units
- Multi-national currency issues
- Multiple entities requiring financial statement consolidation

A number of solid accounting software packages are available for mid-size businesses. You can consult an outside expert to help determine the software system that's right for you, but do not let them push you into a system more complex and costly than you need.

A truly integrated operational and financial system is unlikely to exist at the small to mid-size business level. You will probably still have two systems within the business, and yes, you likely will have some duplication of data between the systems. From a practical standpoint, though, this is still less costly and more efficient than a large "integrated system".

You goal is to find an accounting software system that helps you generate financial statements that are accurate, efficient, and timely, but does not overburden the business financially or operationally.

With the Balance Sheet complete, any Income Statement problems will merely be misclassifications (an item in Miscellaneous Expense that should be in Office Supplies, for example). Some of these items may actually belong in a Balance Sheet account. Thus, a detailed review of each Income Statement account is beneficial during the Balance Sheet Tie-Out process. For instance, some items may be booked in Office Supplies when they are really Office Equipment items that should be capitalized, or some items may be booked in Repairs and Maintenance that should be recorded in Machinery and Equipment.

―IMPORTANT BASE ASSUMPTIONS WITH THIS DISCIPLINE―

1. The organization has a controller or full-charge bookkeeper who is strong enough to carry the financial statements through a solid monthly closing process. This means he or she is able to record all necessary adjusting entries and complete a balance sheet tie-out every month. From this point, the internal accounting system will generate the requisite financial statements.

2. Strong internal controls exist in the financial area of the business. Your organization's internal controls should provide for:
   - Reliability of financial reporting
   - Protection against fraud
   - Compliance with applicable laws and regulations

   This includes appropriate segregation of duties, limited accessibility to cash, basic check points for data entry, timely tax filing, etc. In-depth coverage of internal controls is beyond the scope of this book. Numerous resources are available providing excellent coverage of this topic.

HOW FAST CAN YOU CLOSE?

How quickly you close your month-end accounting period and generate financial statements is determined by a few key timing issues, such as:

- Payroll cycle
- Billing
- Receipt of vendor invoices
- Receipt of bank statements

Seek ways, such as appropriate assumptions and estimates, to accelerate getting this information. Except for year-end close and possibly quarter-end close, accounting staff should be able to push for faster closes even if an estimate or assumption is occasionally off target.

Since financial statements are a lagging indicator, the faster you generate them, the faster you can analyze them and make course corrections. Some companies have even put systems in place to close and generate financial statements just days following month-end.

DISCIPLINE 4:
FINANCIAL ANALYSIS

7

THE OBJECTIVE

The objective of the Financial Analysis is to perform a monthly review and analysis of key financial and operational data following completion of the financial statements. From this analysis, you can effectively complete the next two disciplines, the Narrative Financial Report and the Financial Advisory Review Meeting. We will discuss the five most common types of analysis, but with literally hundreds of analysis methods available, this list is far from exhaustive.

THE APPROACH

To perform the analysis, you need the completed financial statements and any necessary operational data, which depends on the type of analysis you are performing.

Comparative Analysis

Comparative analysis is simply comparing financial and operational results across different time periods, such as:

- This month to this year-to-date
- This month to the same month last year
- This year-to-date to last year-to-date
- Monthly results for all months in the current fiscal year

Your accounting system can likely generate the Income Statement in any of these formats. You should also look at comparative data across time periods for selected Balance Sheet accounts, the Cash Flow Statement, and important operational data. The goal is to identify key fluctuations indicating favorable or unfavorable trends.

Ratio Analysis

Ratio analysis of financial and operational data is critical. Some important ratios are common to many companies. This book will not attempt to list various ratios and assess their value; rather, we will highlight a clearly developed body of knowledge related to ratio analysis. You should apply this comprehensive knowledge on ratios as it relates to the unique needs of your business.

With that in mind, let's consider four common types of financial/operational ratios:

- *Performance Ratios* compare profit performance against the balance sheet (for example, return on invested capital).
- *Leverage Ratios* measure debt to equity to determine the level of financial leverage or risk and the ability to cover the cost of the debt. Examples include debt to equity and average interest cost.
- *Liquidity Ratios* determine the ability of a company to meet short-term liabilities out of short-term cash flow. For example, the current ratio measures the balance of current assets against current liabilities.
- *Activity Ratios* provide comparison measures based on various operational and financial activities within the organization (for example, inventory turns translated into the number of days goods are in inventory).

For more information on specific ratios and their methods of calculation, I recommend *Business Ratios and Formulas: A Comprehensive Guide* by Steven M. Bragg or *Key Management Ratios* by Ciaran Walsh.

Of course, you will need to review any ratios specific to your business or industry. Most companies struggle to pare down the list of key ratios to a workable number, and this only occurs over time. I recommend a final list of 20 or fewer key ratios that are the most meaningful in your business.

Break-Even Analysis

The break-even point for a business is often called a "business ratio" and is used to identify the current break-even point each month. However, a full break-even analysis is more than just the number, as it can be used to perform variance analysis.

Based on your existing break-even point, you can project how much profit you expect at any given revenue level. For a given revenue level, the difference between projected profit and actual profit can be isolated to variances in either cost of goods sold, or selling, general, and administrative expenses. The examination may even include a variance analysis of individual expenses within those areas. You do this by identifying the year-to-date average for each expense and comparing it to the actual expenses for the current month. This makes it easy to highlight items with a significant variance and note the reasons for the variance.

Trend Analysis

Trend analysis compares a consistent metric or ratio over a period of time. Trend analysis could be viewed as a specialized type of comparative analysis, although it typically looks at a larger number of time segments (months, weeks, or days). A simple example would be charting revenue by month over the last three or four years.

The important element to remember with trend analysis is frequency. Technically, it requires six data points to identify a trend. For effective trend analysis, therefore, you either need a frequent measurement or you must measure the metric over a long period of time. Measuring weekly or daily reveals trends much quicker than measuring monthly, but most financial statement analyses follow the monthly rhythm of the financial statements. Therefore, finding reliable trends requires cumulative data from six months or more.

Comparing Actual Results to Projected Results

When comparing actual financial and operational results to projected results, you will always find varying degrees of differences. Therefore, you should identify the significant differences and understand the reasons for them. Among the more meaningful outcomes of this analysis is an increased understanding of the business that leads to better Financial Projections (Discipline 7).

Summary

In addition to reviewing these five common types of analysis, you should also review the most recent Cash Flow Forecast and Smart Number report. This is an easy way to focus your attention on the future rather than the past. The combination of historic-looking Financial Analysis and forward-looking numbers will provide you with the most complete view of your company's financial situation.

PRACTICAL TIPS

1. As you analyze, record your observations in one place. These observations may take the form of questions for further research, concerns requiring action, or rationale about the results. This will provide the basis for the Narrative Financial Report (Discipline 5).

2. Graph the data. Trends are more easily identified when data is presented graphically rather than in tables. With the vast amount of data you'll review each month, short cuts such as graphing make analysis much easier.

3. Spreadsheets are a powerful tool for collecting financial and operational data. With its embedded formulas, new results are quickly calculated simply by entering the current month's data. Such automated analysis leaves more time to examine root causes and determine next actions.

—BENCHMARKING ACROSS DIFFERENT ORGANIZATIONS—

Benchmarking other organizations is a useful analysis. It identifies best-in-class performance to help you set goals for similar or better results. The two most common sources of benchmarking data are:

Third Party Aggregator Financial Comparison Resources

A number of third party aggregator resources of financial comparative information (available in both hard copy and electronic formats) enable you to compare and analyze financial data and ratios by industry category (NAICS) and company size. The data is compiled based on reports from outside sources (e.g., banks, CPA firms) that submit the data sans company identification. One such resource is the Risk Management Association's *RMA Annual Statement Studies: Financial Ratio Benchmarks*. Another is the *ProfitCents* software platform by SageWorks, Inc.

Industry Associations

Many industry associations have benchmarking groups that pull together individual member companies who are similar in size but do not compete geographically with other members. The group then shares financial data – usually filtered and normalized by a third-party entity – for comparison purposes.

Benchmarking analysis can be beneficial, but I offer two notes of caution. First, you must understand what is included in each comparison. If you want to compare gross margins, for example, you must know what expense items are included in cost of goods sold by companies in the comparison study data. It is common to find differences in where some expenses are classified in the Income Statement. As the saying goes, make sure you compare apples to apples.

Second, you must understand that all businesses, even in the same industry, are unique. For example, if your printing business wants to benchmark against other printers of similar size, it's important to know whether the other printers have distribution divisions because they will present a different financial statement and ratio "footprint". The degree of difference depends on the size of the distribution business compared to the size of the printing business. Again, you must make sure you compare apples to apples.

DISCIPLINE 5: NARRATIVE FINANCIAL REPORT 8.

THE OBJECTIVE

Following completion of the Financial Analysis, the Narrative Financial Report summarizes the results and provides context to give a full picture of the company's financial performance and future outlook. Like the Financial Statement Reporting and the Financial Analysis, the Narrative Financial Report should be part of a monthly rhythm. This report should include narrative and graphical elements; readers will better understand and retain the information if they can read and see it rather than stare at tables of numbers.

THE APPROACH

The Narrative Financial Report should answer three fundamental questions:

1. *What* Happened?
2. *So What* Does it Mean?
3. *Now What* Should We Do?

With these questions in mind, I suggest the following framework for the report.

Summary Financial Scorecard
Place a Summary Financial Scorecard (Figure 8.1) on the front page to provide a quick assessment of the four bottom lines: net profit, operating cash flow, return on invested capital, and profit per employee.

Narration of Financial Results
Highlight and explain financial results from the last month using narration and graphics. Focus on key areas, consolidating understanding of the income statement, cash flow statement, and balance sheet for a meaningful story of what happened financially.

Analysis (Financial and Operational)
Summarize the key findings from the Financial Analysis to provide the context for what happened. Operational analysis should also be included. This

section should make abundant use of meaningful graphics.

Comments and Insight
Explain the meaning of the financial story and analysis. Identify as many cause-and-effect relationships as possible. Pull all the pieces together with insightful comments providing the "view of the CFO."

Financial ScoreCard
The Four Bottom Lines for XYZ Company

	Current Month		Year-To-Date		Prior Year	
Summary Income Statement						
Revenue	$1,650,000	100.00%	$15,450,000	100.00%	$18,375,000	100.00%
Cost of Goods Sold	$1,230,000	74.55%	$11,540,000	74.69%	$14,025,000	76.33%
Gross Margin	$420,000	25.45%	$3,910,000	25.31%	$4,350,000	23.67%
Operating Expenses	$275,000	16.67%	$2,650,000	17.15%	$3,000,000	16.33%
Operating Profit (Loss)	$145,000	8.79%	$1,260,000	8.16%	$1,350,000	7.35%
Net Profit (Loss)	**$140,000**	**8.48%**	**$1,185,000**	**7.67%**	**$1,385,000**	**7.54%**

	Current Month		Year-To-Date		Prior Year	
Operating Cash Flow						
Net Profit (Loss)	$140,000		$1,185,000		$1,385,000	
Non-Cash Items						
Depreciation and Amortization	$15,000		$130,000		$145,000	
(Gain) or Loss on Sale of Assets					($5,000)	
Current Balance Sheet Adjustments						
Accounts Receivable	$35,000		($250,000)		($350,000)	
Prepaid Expenses and Deposits	($5,000)		($15,000)		($10,000)	
Accounts Payable	($25,000)		$35,000		($115,000)	
Other Current Liabilities (non-debt)	($10,000)		$25,000		($25,000)	
Operating Cash Flow	**$150,000**		**$1,110,000**		**$1,325,000**	

	Current Month	Year-To-Date	Prior Year
Return on Invested Capital			
Return on Invested Capital	15.57%	17.13%	14.59%

	Current Month	Year-To-Date	Prior Year
Profit Per Employee			
Profit Per Employee (FTE*)	$933	$7,900	$9,893
* FTE = Full Time Equivalent			

Figure 8.1: *The Financial Scorecard provides a quick assessment of the four bottom lines: net profit, operating cash flow, return on invested capital, and profit per employee.*

Investment for the Future
Identify any specific elements of the financial results that relate to conscious investment for the future. This might be as formal as research and development costs or as informal as costs associated with hiring a new salesperson or launching a new geographic territory to grow revenue beyond existing markets. This understanding is healthy so these decisions are properly monitored relative to their expected outcomes.

What to Watch
Note any items in the next several months that require particular attention. Some of this insight may come from reviewing the Smart Numbers.

PRACTICAL TIP

Software is available that embeds various documents – the Narrative Financial Report, analysis spreadsheets, graphs, and financial statements – into one electronic document. This master document can be printed and reviewed in hard copy or distributed electronically. There are many advantages to using such software, including the ability to maintain comprehensive digital archives and reduce paper filing.

Other Elements to Consider

Two additional elements should be included in the Narrative Financial Report for the purpose of generating conversation in the Financial Advisory Review Meeting: unexpected successes and new opportunities.

Unexpected Successes are any successes that surprised the organization. Examples include a new product that is selling better than anticipated or a service that is generating interest and sales from an unexpected market or industry. Unexpected successes are a key source of innovation for the business.

New Opportunities are simply areas where the organization sees a chance to pursue something new and different. The organization should place its best resources – money, talent, and time – in pursuit of the best opportunities.

Neither of these areas are likely to be discovered every single month. In fact, months may go by without significant activity in either area. However, building these topics into the framework of the Narrative Financial Report forces you to think about and discuss them every month. Systematic and proactive work in these areas is essential to the future of your business, so it should be included in the financial management system.

DISCIPLINE 6:
FINANCIAL ADVISORY REVIEW MEETING

9

THE OBJECTIVE

With the Narrative Financial Report complete, you are ready to have a Financial Advisory Review Meeting. Even with a comprehensive and detailed narrative report, this meeting is crucial for generating dialogue that informs future decisions. The management team must discuss potential courses of action and possible ramifications in light of the current financial situation.

THE APPROACH

The review meeting should include the CEO and the senior financial person, whether an internal controller, a CFO, or an outside CFO advisor. (For more on using an outside CFO advisor, see Chapter 12.)

The conversation should focus on the current financial situation, reviewing the narrative financial results and financial analysis, then turn to the remaining five sections of the Narrative Financial Report:

- Comments and Insight
- Investment for the Future
- What to Watch
- Unexpected Successes
- New Opportunities

These sections employ the forward-looking aspects of financial visibility and control and will directly inform financial projections. Decisions facing the CEO can be discussed in context of the financial situation and moved toward meaningful conclusions.

This discipline is simple to describe and understand, but it can be very difficult to execute. It requires significant discipline to schedule and conduct regular face-to-face meetings instead of merely reading the financial statements and Narrative Financial Report. The CEO has the responsibility and vested interest in making sure the meetings happen. They are critical to facilitating meaningful conversation and sound decision-making.

───────────── PRACTICAL TIPS ─────────────

1. Include some educational time in the review meeting. This is a great opportunity to key on one component of the financial statements or financial ratios so that even a CEO with little or no financial background will become fairly adept at understanding them.

2. There may be times when the Financial Advisory Review Meeting extends beyond the CEO. Sometimes there are additional owners who need to be informed of the financial results, or the CEO may choose to include the entire executive team. This, in particular, is a good way to bring a higher level of financial understanding and accountability to other key people in the organization, even if they are not owners.

DISCIPLINE 7: 10
FINANCIAL PROJECTIONS

THE OBJECTIVE

Financial projections allow you to forecast the future financial impact of operating and strategic decisions, using historical financial results to inform the future. This results in a clear sense of visibility and control and is a great way to test your understanding of your company's economic model.

THE APPROACH

We recommend a quarterly financial projection displayed by month. The financial projection should include the Income Statement, Balance Sheet, Cash Flow Statement, and Financial Ratios. Setting up the financial projection format to mirror the line item detail of the monthly financial statements allows you to easily compare the projection to actual results. It also makes it easier to create and maintain the projection model.

Why include financial ratios? Financial statement ratios test the validity of certain assumptions in the model, especially in multi-year financial projections. The common "hockey stick" phenomenon, where revenue and profit growth follows a steep line, is an example of unrealistic forecasting assumptions. For example, in a financial projection for the next two to three years, the revenue-to-fixed asset ratio may be significantly different than in the past, indicating that you have not given enough consideration to the fixed asset acquisitions required to support the projected revenue growth.

PRACTICAL TIPS

1. You can easily extend the quarterly (by month) financial projection model set up in a spreadsheet program to a full twelve months or a multi-year (Year One, Year Two, Year Three, etc.) with a few tweaks in the spreadsheet. This can be useful for providing longer-term projections to banks, investors, etc.

2. Whenever using a spreadsheet, set up check points to confirm the formulas are correct. Formulas commonly become incorrect when lines are added or deleted in a spreadsheet. All formulas should be checked when the model is first created and check figures should be placed throughout the document.

The projection should be created in a spreadsheet model where all of the statements are connected by formulas. This way, a change in one variable on one statement will update the entire model. In addition, you can easily analyze "what if" scenarios by altering the variables to test the expected results. Once you've built the model, updating it is simple, though you should periodically review the formulas and basic assumptions to ensure continued relevancy.

PROJECTIONS VS. BUDGETS

Projections and budgets are somewhat similar, but budgets, typically found in large companies, are fixed financial plans defining the desired spending levels for each area of the business. Projections are more flexible, responding to changes that occur during the quarter or year and adjusting expectations accordingly.

Some companies simply use the projection as a budget for the given quarter or year. A good projection model is easily extended into a flexible budget. Functional leaders – department heads, for example – should be involved in determining the proper allotments for their areas and held accountable for their subsequent performance.

With the projection printed and the budget completed, you can continue using the spreadsheet model for further scenario planning and to modify assumptions as conditions change.

CAN MY SOFTWARE SYSTEM DO PROJECTIONS?

Some accounting software may allow you to input the projection numbers as a "budget" from which you can print reports to compare projection to actual, but most software packages do not have the flexibility required to be the projection model itself. There are certain assumptions and calculations that must be made outside of the financial software. This is where the spreadsheet model is more desirable because it has the ability to do both simple and complex formula structures that more correctly reflect real-life dynamics.

DISCIPLINE 8:
BANK OR INVESTOR PRESENTATION 11

THE OBJECTIVE

Presenting to a bank or investors opens a line of communication regarding the company's financial and strategic performance and future plans. This approach proactively builds and maintains these important relationships. For most mid-size businesses, this is a bank relationship, though some small and mid-size businesses are venture-backed. In those cases, this communication should happen with the outside investors (angel investors, venture capitalists, or private equity groups).

THE APPROACH

The presentation typically follows the final year-end financial statements and review. In a face-to-face meeting with the bank or investors, you should share:

- Historical financial statements
- Financial ratios
- Financial projections for the next one to three years

In addition to the financial package, consider highlighting your business management systems, strategic direction, and specific objectives for the investor relationship. A suggested outline for a portion of the meeting might look like the following:

Business Management Systems

- Financial Management System (highlight the processes you have implemented to increase your financial visibility and control)
- Strategic System (used for strategic planning and execution) such as The CEO Advantage™ (www.theceoadvantage.com)

Strategic Direction

- Dangers
- Opportunities
- Strengths
- Growth Plans

If you are using The CEO Advantage™, you can share your One Page Translator™.

Partnership with Bank/Investor

- Specific Requests
- Relationship (what you would like to see / what they would like to see)
- Reporting Requirements (confirm existing or set new)

―――――――――――――――――PRACTICAL TIP―――――――――――――――――
Sending the financial package in advance of the meeting enables more informed conversation during the meeting.

WHY USE A PART-TIME CFO ADVISOR? 12

The eight disciplines described in this book are not complicated, and a strong controller can oversee the implementation and execution of this system. This process, however, requires you to hold your financial person accountable for delivering the results. The disciplines likely to be the most difficult for a controller, particularly an inexperienced one, to complete are effective financial analysis and meaningful narrative financial reports. CEOs, therefore may want to consider consulting a part-time CFO advisor for two reasons:

- *Balance experience and cost* – Most mid-size businesses cannot justify the $100,000 - $180,000 per year it typically costs for a seasoned CFO. Fortunately, a high level of experience is not usually required on a full-time basis. You can strike a balance by paying for the level and amount of CFO experience you need by hiring a CFO advisor part-time. Yes, a per-time cost premium accompanies an experienced CFO advisor, but the total cost is significantly less than that of a full-time CFO. Some small and mid-size businesses warrant a full-time CFO, including those anticipating significant growth, considering a near-term IPO, or planning to aggressively acquire other companies. More often than not, however, mid-size businesses need CFO-level expertise only on a part-time basis.
- *Obtain an independent and objective viewpoint* - Sometimes you are too close to your business to see certain things, and someone with an outside viewpoint can help clear the view. A CFO advisor also brings experience from working with other clients.

Do You Currently Use an Outside CFO Advisor?

If you currently use an outside CFO advisor, you must hold the CFO advisor accountable for delivering the value of the financial management system like the one described in this book. Other projects may occasionally arise for which you consult a CFO advisor, but the eight disciplines should be the framework for all financial activities. As a result, you will have a strong sense of financial visibility and control, which puts you in a better position to make decisions for your business.

What About My CPA?

Many CPAs position themselves as an outside CFO for their clients; however, this arrangement is often marginalized by a "compliance mindset." CPAs are trained and skilled at resolving compliance issues for financial statement reporting and tax filing. These are important functions for a business and should be performed with excellence. In fact, your bank probably requires a certain level of assurance from a qualified CPA firm before loaning money to your business. In addition, tax planning, reporting, and filing require a CPA's expertise. Beyond this, however, many CPAs lack the operational financial mindset required to think like a CFO. They are not trained to design and implement financial management systems for financial visibility and control.

Another obstacle to using a CPA as an outside CFO is the independence. To maintain the independence required to sign off on financial statements, CPAs cannot be involved in decision-making for the business. This presents difficulties for the CPA when the CEO requires specific financial opinions and decisions of the type a CFO would provide.

I Already Have a CFO

If you already have a CFO, you may not feel you need a CFO advisor. Sometimes, however, those with the title of CFO are actually only performing the tasks of a controller. Is your CFO providing the elements of the eight disciplines? Do you have clear financial visibility and control of your business, or are you struggling with a financial blind spot?

Many CFOs were trained as CPAs and, as already discussed, are disproportionately focused on compliance. Once they drop the monthly financial statement on the CEO's desk, they resume recording transactions, filing tax reports, and ensuring compliance with various agencies. While these tasks are necessary, they can easily be done by less experienced and lower paid financial staff. With a proper understanding of the disciplines described in this book, compliance-minded CFOs can implement a comprehensive financial management system for greater financial visibility and control.

I Already Have a Controller

The advice for "I already have a CFO" applies here, as well. By understanding the disciplines described in this book, a controller can implement a comprehensive financial management system for greater financial visibility and control. Many controllers, however, lack the experience to implement and maintain all eight disciplines, specifically disciplines four through eight. An experienced CFO advisor can guide them in developing the skills and insight necessary for their role.

RECOMMENDED RESOURCES 13

All business owners should educate themselves on financial statements and overall financial management. I have found the following resources to be especially helpful.

Managing By the Numbers: A Commonsense Guide to Understanding and Using Your Company's Financials
Chuck Kremer and Ron Rizzuto with John Case (2000) – developed in partnership with *Inc* magazine

This is an excellent resource for learning the basic uses and limitations of financial statements, as well as understanding how each of them is constructed. Their concept of the three bottom lines is foundational to business financial analysis and should be understood by all businesses beyond the sole-proprietor level.

Another great concept in this book is the Financial Scoreboard/Mobley Matrix™. Developed years ago by IBM executive Lou Mobley, the Mobley Matrix™ is an invaluable tool for learning how financial statements relate to each other, moving from the beginning balance sheet to the ending balance sheet by way of the income statement and cash flow statement. However, the format has practical limitations. In my opinion, it's better to teach with the framework, then focus on the actual financial statements, the financial scorecard with the four bottom lines (net profit, operating cash flow, return on invested capital and net profit per employee) and any additional financial analysis pertinent to the business.

Cash Rules: Learn and Manage the 7 Cash-Flow Drivers for Your Company's Success
Bill McGuinness (2000) – from Kiplinger's Business Management Library

This book is for the business owner who has a fairly good grasp of financial statements and how they flow together. While it covers the basics of financial statements and some definitions of related terms (including the difference between the frequently confused *gross margin* and *contribution margin*), its real impact is in explaining the seven cash flow drivers.

One great tool from this book is the Uniform Credit Analysis®, a bank loan cash flow analysis spreadsheet. This is the primary spreadsheet used by commercial bankers, a group intensely interested in cash flow, and every business owner should understand it. An understanding of the tools and thought processes of commercial bankers is invaluable when preparing presentations for your own commercial banker.

This book also explains the two sides of gross margin: (1) increasing the real and perceptual value equation, and (2) rigorous cost control, much of which comes from reducing errors and non-value-added steps in the operating process.

The New Metrics of Corporate Performance: Profit Per Employee
Lowell Bryan – from McKinsey Quarterly, First Quarter 2007, adapted from his book, *Mobilizing Minds: Creating Wealth from Talent in the 21st Century*, McGraw-Hill, 2007

This article builds the case for *net profit per employee* as the best metric for knowledge-based businesses. Rather than basing performance measures on capital investment, this metric measures return on talent, which is increasingly applicable to our 21st century post-industrial economy. Mr. Bryan actually does refer to net profit per employee in connection with return on capital, but he suggests the return on capital measure is "largely a sanity check." I also believe they are connected, and, along with net profit and operating cash flow, undergird the four bottom lines.

In a couple of places the article mentions that net profit per employee is preferable because of how easy it is to obtain the number of employees making the metric less subject to the "vagaries of accounting definitions" and other corporate-finance decisions than return on capital. While I somewhat agree, I offer two counterpoints.

First, while determining the number of employees seems easy, it is also subject to vagaries. *Employee* is a legal term, and organizations increasingly employ talent outside of the legal definition of *employee,* including part-time workers, seasonal workers, contract workers, and free agents. Management can therefore manipulate the number of employees accordingly. Determining the "full-time equivalent" for number of employees is subject to assumption and estimation.

Second, the numerator in the metric is net profit, which, similar to return on capital, has its own share of "vagaries" based on accounting definitions and corporate finance decisions. Indeed, every metric has limitations, which is why I suggest the four bottom lines. Each provides a complementary piece to the complete financial picture.

ABOUT THE AUTHOR & CREDITS

About the Author

Troy D. Schrock, CPA, is the developer of The Action CFO Process™. The Action CFO Process is used by independent CFO advisors to deliver the Action CFO Financial Visibility and Control System™ for business owners. Mr. Schrock has been an independent CFO advisor since 1997.

Before becoming an independent CFO advisor, Mr. Schrock was a manager in a CPA firm in Southfield, Michigan. During his time in public accounting, Mr. Schrock was privileged to work with entrepreneurial businesses from start-up through mid-market as an advisor in tax, accounting, and business valuation issues.

Mr. Schrock graduated from the University of Illinois with a Bachelor of Science in Accountancy. He lives in southeast Michigan with his wife and three children and devotes his time to three primary passions – the Bible, business, and lifetime effectiveness.

Mr. Schrock can be reached at *troy.schrock@actioncfo.com.*

Credits

I am grateful for the opportunity to create this resource for the benefit of CEOs in growing mid-size businesses and the CFO advisors who assist them. The diligent efforts of the editing staff have been invaluable in shaping the final product, and I am indebted to them for their skills. Specifically, Scott Bahr has proven himself indispensable as an editor and capable in handling the many important details in producing the final product you now hold in your hands. In addition, I appreciate Joe Leman's expertise in developing the cover and interior graphics.

I owe a special note of thanks to the clients with whom I have enjoyed working over the years as a CFO advisor. These engagements have helped me to refine the ideas expressed in this resource. More importantly, these are not just professional, but personal relationships built on mutual respect and trust. I look forward to continuing our work together.

Of course, any project like this pulls time from family. I am blessed to have a wonderful wife and three precious children who support my commitment to my work.

Ultimate thanks belong to God and His Son, Jesus Christ, for entrusting me with the talent and opportunity to pursue my passions in a way that aligns with my values and strengths. May all that I do be performed with excellence to His Glory.

Do you see a man who excels in his work? He will stand before kings; he will not stand before unknown men. Proverbs 22:29

www.ingramcontent.com/pod-product-compliance
Lightning Source LLC
Chambersburg PA
CBHW040846180526
45159CB00001B/337